Whose BOTTOM Is This?

Written and Photographed by
Wayne Lynch

Gareth Stevens Publishing
A WORLD ALMANAC EDUCATION GROUP COMPANY

Please visit our web site at: **www.garethstevens.com**
For a free color catalog describing Gareth Stevens Publishing's
list of high-quality books and multimedia programs, call
1-800-542-2595 (USA) or 1-800-387-3178 (Canada).
Gareth Stevens Publishing's fax: (414) 332-3567.

Library of Congress Cataloging-in-Publication Data

Lynch, Wayne.
     Whose bottom is this? / written and photographed by Wayne Lynch.
          p. cm. — (Name that animal!)
     Includes bibliographical references and index.
     Summary: Asks the reader to identify various animals from descriptions
of their rear ends and provides information about the physical characteristics
and behavior of each animal.
     ISBN 0-8368-3639-1 (lib. bdg.)
     1. Buttocks—Juvenile literature. 2. Animals—Juvenile literature.
(1. Animals. 2. Buttocks.) I. Title.
QL950.39.L96 2003
591.4'1—dc21   2002036525

This edition first published in 2003 by
Gareth Stevens Publishing
A World Almanac Education Group Company
330 West Olive Street, Suite 100
Milwaukee, Wisconsin 53212 USA

This U.S. edition © 2003 by Gareth Stevens, Inc. Original edition © 2000
by Wayne Lynch. First published in 2000 by Whitecap Books, Vancouver.
Additional end matter © 2003 by Gareth Stevens, Inc.

Photograph on page 3 by Aubrey Lang

Gareth Stevens series editor: Dorothy L. Gibbs
Gareth Stevens graphic designer: Katherine A. Goedheer

Printed in the United States of America

1 2 3 4 5 6 7 8 9 07 06 05 04 03

While you are reading this book, you are probably sitting on your bottom. People usually do not like to show their bare bottoms, so they wear clothes to cover them.

Wild animals do not wear clothes, so their bottoms are always showing. The bottoms of wild animals come in many different shapes and colors. Some wild animal bottoms are bright. Some are beautiful. Some are big.

Can you name the wild animals whose bottoms are pictured in this book?

Even at a young age, I have short, pudgy legs and a wide, round bottom — like my mother. I am chubby because I eat for many hours every night. I have a big mouth and strong lips, so I can clip grass like a lawn mower. My unusual name means "river horse," but no horse ever looked like me!

Who am I?

I am a hippopotamus. I live in the lakes and rivers of tropical Africa. In the water, young hippos like me stay close to their mothers for protection from hungry crocodiles. During the day, we sleep in the water and rest our heads on our mothers' backs.

A hippopotamus has no hair on its body. Its thick brownish-gray skin produces a special pink fluid that protects it from sunburn.

A beautiful fan of shiny feathers makes mine one of the prettiest bottoms in the bird world. Every spring, males like me gather in groups to dance and show off. We try to get the females to notice us by puffing up our chests and making funny popping noises. The best "poppers" attract the most females.

Who am I?

I am a sage grouse. I live on the prairies of North America. In winter, I eat mainly the leaves of sagebrush plants, which is how I got my name. In summer, I also eat wildflowers, grass seeds, and certain insects. Coyotes and bobcats are some of the animals that would like to eat me.

A sage grouse is about the same size as a small wild turkey. Its legs are covered with feathers to keep them warm in winter.

I was born on an island of ice floating in the sea. When I am resting on the ice, I fold my back flippers together. They look like two big, furry hands covering my bottom. Although I live in a very cold place, I stay warm because I have thick fur covering my skin and a thick layer of fat, called blubber, under my skin.

Who am I?

I am a harp seal pup. I live in the icy cold waters of the Arctic. My mother's milk is thicker than whipping cream, so I grow fat very quickly. When I am only two weeks old, my mother leaves me, and I must take care of myself. When I first start to swim, I eat tiny shrimp. Later, I catch fish to eat.

A harp seal pup has very large eyes to help it see in the darkness underwater.

I have tough, wrinkled skin. It protects me from sharp thorns when I run through the bushes. When I feel itchy, I like to rub my bottom against tree trunks and termite mounds. Rubbing sometimes leaves scratches on my bottom. I am a very big animal. I can grow to weigh as much as a small car.

Who am I?

I am a white rhinoceros. I live in Africa. I am very strong, so nothing frightens me. I use the long horn on the end of my snout to protect myself against dangerous lions and hyenas. Over many years, my horn could grow to be longer than a baseball bat.

A rhinoceros has no front teeth. It uses its strong lips to tear off grass to eat. Grass is a rhinoceros's favorite food.

My two buddies and I have to paddle hard with our webbed feet to keep our bottoms in the air. We are trying to eat snails, insects, worms, and roots that live and grow underwater. When summer is over, we will lose our long pointed tails. We will lose the black feathers on our bottoms, too, and grow plain brown ones for winter.

Who am I?

I am a male pintail duck. I live on the small lakes and marshes of North America, Europe, and Asia. My female partner has plain brown feathers all year round. They help her hide from foxes and coyotes as she sits on the eight creamy yellow eggs she lays in spring.

Mother pintail ducks raise their ducklings alone. They make their nests on the ground, often far from the nearest water.

My bright white bottom can be seen from far away, so other animals know where I am. In summer, I live high in the mountains, where I eat grass and wildflowers in mountain meadows. I live in a group called a band. All of the animals in the band watch out for predators, such as wolves, coyotes, and mountain lions.

Who am I?

I am a bighorn sheep. I live in the mountains of western North America. A male like me is called a ram. A female is called a ewe. My horns are bigger and stronger than the horns of a ewe. When I fight with other rams, we stand on our hind legs and smash our heads together.

Bighorn sheep love salt. In winter, they sometimes eat the salt that is put on highways to melt the ice.

I probably have the most dangerous bottom of any animal. Underneath my golden fur, I have many sharp quills. Some of them are longer than your fingers. I have quills all over my body, except on my face and my belly. When a mountain lion wants to eat me, I just turn my back toward it and show it how scary I can be.

Who am I?

I am a porcupine. I live in the forests of North America. I have a quiet life. I spend most of the day sleeping inside a cave or a hollow tree. At night, I climb trees to eat. In winter, I mainly eat tree bark. In summer, leaves, buds, and fruits are my favorite foods.

Baby porcupines are called porcupettes. They are born with soft quills, but their quills quickly harden.

Index

More Books to Read

Animal Tails. David M. Schwartz (Gareth Stevens)

Bottoms Up: A Book About Rear Ends. Marilyn Singer (Henry Holt)

Tails That Talk and Fly. Diane Swanson (Greystone Books)

Telling Tails. Rookie Read-About Science (series). Allan Fowler (Children's Press)